I love how the questions really dig into Joseph's life and experiences. I enjoyed relating them to our own lives, and the study helped me dig into my life to find the tough stuff I have been through. I learned how we can choose to respond in each season and how God created seasons to grow you into all He has made you to be.

—Jenn Carlson, wife, mom of three, nonprofit missions director

Women will benefit from doing this study in a small group setting by building community, deepening relationships, and establishing support systems. Women can more easily lean into the season they are in if they know what the season is. We have a great model in Joseph's life of embracing each season and growing closer to God and our destiny through the seasons.

—Nika Davis, wife, mom of four, dentist

This study will help women understand how the seasons of life have different purposes and are all necessary. The study requires transparency and creates deep bonds within the group. It also helps you reflect on your own life and the trials and tribulations you have encountered.

—Emily S., wife, mom of three, community developer

SEASONS

of a

WOMAN'S SOUL

Discover God's Purpose in Your Life Story

JENNY MCJUNKIN

WESTBOW
PRESS®
A DIVISION OF THOMAS NELSON
& ZONDERVAN

WestBow Press books may be ordered through booksellers or by contacting:

WestBow Press
A Division of Thomas Nelson & Zondervan
1663 Liberty Drive
Bloomington, IN 47403
www.westbowpress.com
1 (866) 928-1240

Interior Image Credit: Diane Egge

ISBN: 978-1-9736-5560-2 (sc)
ISBN: 978-1-9736-5562-6 (hc)
ISBN: 978-1-9736-5561-9 (e)

Library of Congress Control Number: 2019902629

Print information available on the last page.

WestBow Press rev. date: 5/13/2019

SEASONS
of a
WOMAN'S
SOUL

To Mom, for following faithfully after Jesus. I have spent my whole life walking in your footsteps.

Contents

About the Author

Jenny McJunkin is a full-time wife, mother, licensed minister, author, and speaker. She served on college campuses ministering to students with Chi Alpha Ministries for a decade.

She writes and speaks about the importance of rest and simplifying life, her failed attempt at homeschooling, the heartbreak of having a child with special needs, and her love for reaching people for Jesus. She openly shares her struggle to pursue a balanced life in our fast-paced world and encourages women everywhere to create space for God's rest and community.

Jenny enjoys drinking coffee, running, and raising all types of animals (horses, tortoises, pigs, chickens, cats, dogs, lizards, hamsters, fish, frogs, and anything else she can find on Craigslist). She resides in Scottsdale, Arizona, with her husband, Tory, and their five rambunctious kids: Josiah, Grace, Judah, Lincoln, and Levi.

Engage with Jenny at jennymcjunkin.com and follow her parenting blog at porchswingmom.com.

Introduction

Life was full and productive. I was leading a bustling campus ministry with weekly large-group meetings, small-group Bible studies, prayer times, retreats, campus outreaches, events, international mission trips and a constant influx of new students. I was speaking at national large-group meetings, regional meetings, churches, and conferences. It was an exciting, fulfilling whirlwind.

In the middle of all the commotion, I started dating Tory. We became best friends, fell deeply in love, and quickly got married. I transitioned out of my ministry and moved to another state to join my husband during his medical training. Together, in short time, we moved to Iowa, Texas, and Minnesota before we settled in Scottsdale, Arizona. Soon afterward, we welcomed the birth of our first two children, Josiah and Grace. I found myself in a new city, at a new church, making new friends. I had a new life and traded the busyness of ministry for the chaos and loneliness of a stay-at-home mom caring for two young children.

I felt restless and was searching for my next big ministry role when the Holy Spirit whispered, "You are in a winter season." At the time, I had no idea what this could be. I thought, *What is a winter season?* As I studied the life of Joseph, God revealed to me His design of seasons in nature and the correlation with seasons in our lives.

Different seasons of our souls are intentionally created, and there are specific reasons and purposes for each season. As much as we want endless summer fun, we can't have it. It wouldn't produce good fruit in our lives. Trees, gardens, and all of creation need time to rest. There is a God-designed cycle and rhythm in nature, and there is a God-designed rhythm in our lives as well; we just need to recognize it. Understanding the seasons and the purpose of each season changed me and allowed me to embrace and thrive in the quietness of being a stay-at-home mom.

A few years later, I gathered a group of women and led this study for the first time. It formed powerful and deep friendships. Many of us continued to meet weekly for the next eight years. This past year, I revised the study and led it again with my small group. Again, the experience was rich and empowering. I knew it was time to publish it so more women could discover their seasons and thrive.

In this study, women will find rest and freedom as they understand the different seasons of their lives. There is a time and season for everything. God takes us through many transitions physically, spiritually, and emotionally. Our lives are like the seasons of nature; each one has a purpose and was created to accomplish different things. We don't want to be a tree sending buds out during the chill of winter, and we don't want to hang on to the joy of summer when God shifts our lives and calls us into a fall transition. Some seasons are difficult, which we see very clearly in the life of Joseph, but each one has a God purpose.

This study was created in a winter season. No one knew who I was or what I had done before becoming a mom. Although I exhausted myself every day, I received no recognition like I had previously as a public speaker and minister. At first, I thought winter was boring and difficult, but I learned to love it. It's quiet on the surface, but beneath the surface, my roots were growing deeper. I was developing depth and strength of character. My visible productivity was on hold, but God was working in His quiet and unseen ways. I found the freedom to rest and embrace my season, and it changed my life!

This study will foster an incredible time of insight and personal growth for every person who partakes. The final week of the study will bring revelation to your life in a powerful way. You will each create and share your personal Seasons Timeline. You will be blown away as you see the hand of God so carefully guiding your life. You will see with clarity how the painful and dark times are leading us to new and wonderful places through God's strategic and loving plan. You will finish the study with hearts connected deeply to each other and the overwhelming confidence in God's goodness.

I can't tell you how excited I am for you to go through *Seasons of a Woman's Soul*! It will open your eyes to see more of God in your daily life, and it will help you deeply connect with other women. We are each in a season of life, and God has an ordained purpose for each season. He has a beautiful plan and specific lessons to teach each one of us. Gather new and old friends for this study, discover together what season of life you are in, and learn how to thrive in that season. Is it time to rest? Time to plant? Time to bloom? Your life will be enriched as you gain insights into your seasons and see God's amazing plan for your life unfolding in front of your eyes!

Love,
Jenny

How to Make the Most of This Study

Simple suggestions to help you rock this study:

- Have everyone bring their own copy of the study so they can write in their answers, journal, and create their personal timeline.
- No preparation is needed! The study is ready to pick up and go. Everything is laid out for you. Simply turn to week 1 and start reading the questions.
- We learn the most when we share. We want vibrant sharing and connecting. Through dialogue, the richness of the topic will develop. Insight will bubble up as women listen to one another's perspectives and learn from each other.
- There are no right or wrong answers in this study. Many questions do not have concrete answers, and responses may vary, such as, "How do you think Joseph felt when he was thrown in prison?" We have no way to really know exactly how he felt,

but we draw on how we would feel if we were in Joseph's place.

- Busy, busy, busy? No problem! The recommended scripture reading only takes about five minutes the night before the study. I highly recommend reading the scriptures once before group. However, I know how life can usurp your good intentions, and if you don't find the chance to read before group, you will read the scriptures together during the study. Never miss a group because you didn't have time to read beforehand. Everything is covered during group.

- If you have four or more women in your study, you will want to break into smaller groups for the reflection questions and prayer. The smaller groups should be two or three women, which fosters guards being dropped and increased intimacy.

- Save the last ten or fifteen minutes for sharing in smaller groups and praying for each other. You will see some beautiful prayer times here. Shy people often will feel comfortable enough to pray in a group of three people, but they might never pray in front of the whole group. Make your prayer time personal—and get in close to each other. Put a hand on your friend's shoulder, hold hands or put your arms around each other, and hug. It's a beautiful time when the Holy Spirit sweeps in and heals hearts, pours out love, comforts us, and knits our hearts together. The atmosphere will be primed for prayer all through the study, and the ensuing prayers are honest, gentle, and full of compassion and power. You will see prayers answered and lives changed!

For the Facilitator Only

- Facilitate intimacy and engage in the study. Everyone, including the facilitator, needs to jump in and learn along with everyone else. Share your heart, cry, laugh, and just be one of the girls.
- As the facilitator, be first to answer the first two questions each week. These are the introductory questions. You will set the tone for all other answers, and the other women will follow your example. Also, when you answer first, you will have better control of pacing the group through the study and making sure you end on time.
- *Seasons of a Woman's Soul* is intentionally designed to be super easy for the facilitator. Since you already have to clean your dorm room, apartment, or house, provide a snack and remind the women to come. That's enough work and preparation time! It's recommended (but optional, depending on your group) for the ladies to read the scriptures ahead of time. However, if they just show up, that's completely okay. If reading or homework for the study is a requirement, you run the risk of women

not coming to the study if they didn't have time to read the material in advance. Encourage everyone to just show up even if it's in their pajamas. Always welcome people even in their rawest form and be a safe place for them.

- Text a reminder each time before your group meets. List the day and time for group and ask them to read the scriptures you will be discussing. Take five minutes to read the scriptures and pray for your study. You are all set!

- You don't have to teach. They will learn the most when they dialogue and discuss the questions. This study is designed for everyone to learn from each other. This happens naturally as women answer the questions and share their perspectives and insights.

- I use three methods of drawing answers out of women:

  1. Go around in a circle. Everyone answers the question. I would do this during the introductory questions.
  2. Popcorn method. Ask the question and wait for people to answer. Let two or three people answer, offer your own insight, and then move on to the next question if there is silence. If the discussion is good, stay on the topic longer.
  3. Call on people. Occasionally direct a person to share, especially someone who hasn't shared much that day. Remember that everyone wants to share.

- Sharing: Week 6 will be your favorite week, and it is a fantastic, love-filled way to begin wrapping up *Seasons of a Woman's Soul*. Each woman needs about fifteen minutes to share. Consider how long it will take (given the number of women attending) for everyone to share. (If you have five or fewer women, each person can share for twenty minutes. If you have more than five, you will only have time for each woman to share for fifteen minutes.) Select a designated timer. Give each woman fifteen minutes. Ask the timer to hold up a "one-minute reminder" card before the time is up. It is too easy for one person to share for thirty minutes—and you don't want to run out of time before everyone has had time to share.
- Prepare for fluctuating attendance. The best thing you can do is to be consistent. Women are busy, overwhelmed, and overcommitted. Women will skip and miss your group. It's not you, and it's not the study; it's our culture. And women desperately need your consistency and the safe place of connection you are creating.
- When someone misses, reach out to them to let them know they were missed. Ask how you can pray for them. Make them feel loved and cared for—and never make them feel bad or guilty for missing. Be consistent and loving, and you will have a great study.

Week 1

FALL~
TRANSITION

change LETTING GO dying **end**
of production saying goodbye
death of a dream preparation for
winter *loss* **disappointment**

Unless a grain of wheat falls into the ground and dies, it remains alone; but if it dies, it produces much fruit.

—John 12:24

Introduction to Fall

God designed each season with careful thought and purpose. We have four distinct seasons, and not one of them is more or less significant than the others. We begin our study of Joseph with his fall season. Fall is a season of transition and change. God positioned autumn as a bridge between the production of summer and the rest of winter.

In the high plains of Wyoming, where I lived half my life, fall comes on suddenly. One week, we are having a picnic in the grass, and the next week, a cold wind blows in with unexpected flurries to announce the season has changed. In nature, growth slows—and the trees and bushes stop producing fruit and flowers. The flowers dry up on sticklike stems. The colors change, a beautiful death of leaves. Nature begins her transition. She lets go of the busyness of summer and the days of productivity and orients herself toward quieter and calmer days.

A fall season of the soul correlates with a season of transition and change in our lives. Maybe you say goodbye to your friends and move to a new state or transition from studies to a career. Maybe you take a break from working full-time in an office to begin a season as a stay-at-home mom. Maybe the relationship you thought would last forever ends. Fall is a transition time in our lives, a time of loss, sadness, grief, and letting go of what we had before. Fall often represents the death of a dream in our lives. A hope we carried in our hearts must now be allowed to rest. It can be emotionally difficult and often devastating, a season we try to avoid if we can. However, God has a purpose for our fall seasons.

Although it can be painful and confusing, God is in the middle of it, using everything for our good. God uses our fall seasons of transition to lead us to new destinations—places of purpose and influence.

Bible Study

- Say your name, your favorite season, and why you like it.

- When looking at nature, what happens in fall?

A Look at Joseph

Read Genesis 37:1–36.

- What things did Joseph lose in this life transition?

- What kinds of emotions do you think Joseph experienced when he arrived in his new home?

- How did he respond?

- How could Joseph have responded?

- What attitudes of the heart do you think the Lord was working on? Key verse: "Unless a grain of wheat falls into the ground and dies, it remains alone; but if it dies, it produces much fruit" (John 12:24). The "grain of wheat" is our dreams, hopes, and plans; "dies" means death or letting go; and "produces fruit" references our need for fall to prepare for the next summer and fruitful seasons of life.

- How does this verse relate to fall?

- How did Joseph get through this difficult time? What did he put his hope in? Jeremiah 29:11 says, "I know the thoughts I have toward you, says the

Lord, thoughts of peace and not of evil, to give you a future and a hope."

- How does this verse encourage us during the hard seasons of life? "The Lord was with Joseph, the Lord gave him favor with Potiphar, the Lord blessed him" (Genesis 39:1–4).

Fall Response Questions

Discuss in groups of three.

How can you recognize when you are in a fall season?

What should you do if you are in fall?

What pitfalls should you be aware of?

What can you put your hope in during this season?

Share a time when you had a difficult life transition or had to let go of what you were familiar with.
Where was God in your loss?

Close

Close by praying for God to heal the pain we have experienced from our losses.

Looking Ahead

In preparation for next week's study, please read Genesis 39:1–20.

Journal

Week 2

WINTER~
REST

Quiet stillness **anonymous** unseen
growth *hibernation* unproductive NO
PUBLIC ACCOMPLISHMENTS *waiting*
no accolades dormant

For six years you are to sow your fields and harvest the crops, but during the seventh year let the land lie unplowed and unused.
—Exodus 23:10–11a (NIV)

Introduction to Winter

When you look out across a winter landscape after a fresh snowfall, everything seems muted. There are no green leaves on the trees or colorful blooms on the rose bushes; the grass is brown and dormant. It is very difficult to tell from observation if a tree is alive or dead. Although there are no signs of growth, trees are very much alive in winter. They are resting. Much of nature is sleeping— bears, reptiles, and gardens are all dormant. Production takes high amounts of energy, and winter is the perfect balance to a busy summer. It is quiet, growth is unseen and unnoticed, and yet life is there! Beneath the surface, the roots are searching out water to sustain life. God created winter intentionally for creation to rest, recover, and be strengthened.

Winter of the soul has a parallel purpose. It is a time where we may feel unproductive, a time of waiting, stillness, and quiet. You may not receive applause or recognition for your work. It may feel like you are not accomplishing anything or making any progress toward your life dreams or goals. Yet winter is a season to be embraced. It is designed by God for rest and for unseen growth.

In winter, roots grow stronger and deeper in nature and in our lives as well. As nature rests, it is restored. Winter in the soul is often where we process our transition. We seek God for meaning in our disappointments and listen while we wait for His direction. A winter season is given to us by design, for rest from the pressure and performance of external work. Winter is a season to help us grow deeper roots in our internal lives and our souls. If we allow it, God will strengthen our character and clarify our vision in winter. Embrace winter. It is a gift of rest for the body, mind, and soul. The winter season is the perfect balance to the productivity of summer. Quiet down, deepen your roots, and you will see and hear all God is doing in your soul during winter.

Bible Study

- Say your name and share the last time you did something restful and what it was.

- Are you good at resting? Why or why not?

Returning to Joseph

Review

- Who can recap what we learned about fall last week?

- Where did we leave off in the story of Joseph?

Read Genesis 39:1–20, in which Joseph is thrown in prison.

Winter is for character development.

- Does personal suffering reveal our character or perfect it?

- How do you work through an injustice?

- Would you be angry with God?

- How did Joseph resolve this?

- Did Joseph need so suffer?

- What did Joseph's heart go through in the darkness of prison?

Winter is for rest.

Joseph spent between five and ten years in prison.

- What did he do while he was in prison?

- What did he focus on during these years?

- What was the purpose?

- What does God think about unproductive seasons of life? Read Exodus 20:8–11.

- What is a Sabbath, and why did God create it? Read Exodus 23:10–12. In the seventh year, the fields were not plowed or cultivated. Land was left fallow for a season or more.

- What do gardens do in the winter? What do trees do? What do grizzly bears do? What do ants do?

- Do trees lose their leaves to survive the winter—or did God create winter to give trees a break from continual growth?

- Does sleep have a purpose?

- Read Mark 6:31. What do we learn from this verse?

- What did Jesus, God's perfect Son, do in his twenties?

Winter Response Questions

Discuss in groups of three.

- How can you recognize when you are in a winter season?
- What should you do?
- What temptations might you have?
- What key things are accomplished in winter (character, rest, establishing a good foundation)?
- Making it personal: Have you had a season of rest? Why or why not? Are you in winter now?

Close

Close by praying for each other to find times of rest and refreshment this week and for any additional prayer requests.

Looking Ahead

For next week, please read Genesis 29:20–23 and Genesis 40:1–23.

Journal

Week 3

SPRING~
INVESTING

Plowing **planting** *waiting* working
hard more waiting ***hope*** new
beginnings *seeds* vision

Let us not become weary in doing good, for at the proper time we will reap a harvest if we do not give up.

—Galatians 6:9

Introduction to Spring

Spring is a season for investing in our future. It is a season of new beginnings, a season of hope and vision. The stillness and rest of winter begins to fade, and the weather warms up. Hope fills our hearts. We dream again, new dreams. It's not a revival of what we lost through our fall transition.

We no longer entertain the hope of regaining what we lost; a new vision is forming in our hearts. Spring is the season when we plant seeds in our gardens, seeds of dreams and seeds of destiny. We work hard and steadily. We are plowing, planting, investing, sowing, dreaming, and being faithful to the work before us. After we plant, we wait. We continue to be faithful wherever we are and in whatever position we hold. After you plant, the earth continues to remain bare for a time. There are no signs of new life. There is only our hope that the seeds will sprout and our lives will finally bear new fruit.

Bible Study

- Share a time when you really worked hard toward a goal. What was it? What steps did you have to take to reach your goal?

- Have you ever had a new beginning? What was it?

Review

- Who can summarize what we learned about winter last week?

- Where did we leave off in our story of Joseph?

Spring is for investing and planting seeds for our future. We are in a major transition again, but this time, it is from the rest of winter into the fruitfulness of summer.

Read Genesis 39:20–23.

- What do we see Joseph doing?

- How is he investing in his future?

Read 1 Corinthians 10:31: "So whether you eat or drink or whatever you do, do it all for the glory of God."

Read Galatians 6:9: "Let us not become weary in doing good, for at the proper time we will reap a harvest if we do not give up."

- How do these verses apply to a spring season?

Read Genesis 40:1–23.

The butler and the baker have dreams.

- How is Joseph investing in his future through this encounter?

- How did the interaction with the butler and baker infuse hope into Joseph?

- What do we need in order to plant?

Read Proverbs 20:4: "Sluggards do not plow in season; so at harvest time they look but find nothing."

- What happens if we don't plant in the spring?

Read Genesis 41:1.

Two years went by, and Pharaoh had a dream. Joseph waited two years after the butler and the baker.

- Why do you think God make Joseph wait so long?

- What happens to us while we wait?

Springtime is for new beginnings. Justice and redemption are coming!

Read Genesis 41:1–41.

Joseph's Rise to Power

Joseph was thirty years old when Pharaoh put him in charge of everything.

- How old was Joseph when God first gave him his dreams of the moon and stars bowing down and the grains of wheat bowing down?

- Joseph's rise to power seems sudden, but was it? Where did he get his training to successfully lead the nation of Egypt?

Spring Response Questions

Discuss in groups of three.

- How can you recognize when you are in a spring season?

- What should you do?

- What temptations might you have?

- What key things are accomplished in spring?

Making It Personal

- What fills you with hope?

- How are you investing in your future?

Close

Close by praying for each other and the dreams you have for your future.

Looking Ahead

Please read Genesis 41:40–57; 42:1–9.

Journal

Week 4

SUMMER ~ FRUITFULNESS

Enjoyment **nourishment** fruit *goals*

achieved success **praise** public
recognition ACCOMPLISHMENTS,

rewards destiny fulfilled

Introduction to Summer

Summer is a season of fruitfulness. It is a season where we have achieved our goals and are living our destinies. It is a time of accomplishments and recognition. Summer is the season where we feel we are hitting our stride in life and doing what we were created to do. It's a wonderful time. Our confidence is high, and we are reaping the rewards of all our labors.

The seeds we planted in the spring have flourished into healthy plants that are producing abundant fruits and vegetables. We have increased clarity on our fall and winter seasons, and we can see how God used all our difficult times for our good—and also for the good of others. Our time of suffering is over, and we embrace summer with confidence, joy, and thankfulness for all God has brought us through. "And the name of the second he called Ephraim: 'For God has caused me to be fruitful in the land of my affliction'" (Genesis 41:52 NKJV).

Bible Study

- How do you feel when you think about summer?

- Share a time when you felt like you were "in your element" or doing what you were created to do.

Review

- Where did we leave off in our story of Joseph?

Dreams Fulfilled

We are rewarded and experience God's favor and blessings.

Read Genesis 41:40–57.

- How is Joseph tangibly rewarded for his faithfulness during his fall, winter, and spring seasons? Power, wife, clothing, rings, gold/wealth, recognition, favor with rulers and kings, title, position, children, and healing.

- How do you think Joseph is feeling during this season of his life?

Read Genesis 41:52 again.

- What is Joseph's attitude toward God's blessings?

- What should our response be during seasons of God's blessings and favor on our lives?

Read Genesis 42:1–9.

Dreams Fulfilled

Joseph remembered his dreams about his brothers.

- How many years had gone by since God had given him the dreams of his brothers bowing down to him? At least twenty years.

- What can we learn about God's timing versus our timing when it comes to the dreams God has put in our hearts?

Read Ecclesiastes 3:1–8.

A Time for Everything

Summer gives us perspective on our fall season. We see God's hand in our circumstances, and we see His faithfulness.

- Why do we want to live in continual summer?

- Why is this not a realistic approach to life?

Read Genesis 45:1–9.

Joseph reveals his identity to his brothers. "So it was not you who send me here but God" (Genesis 45:8).

"And we know that all things work together for good to those who love God, to those who are called according to His purpose" (Romans 8:28).

- What do these two verses reveal about God's character?

"But as for you, you meant evil against me; but God meant it for good, in order to bring it about as it is this day, to keep many people alive" (Genesis 50:20).

- How did Joseph come to this conclusion through all the injustice and suffering He endured?

- How can we gain perspective on our fall and winter seasons?

Summer Response Questions

Discuss in groups of three.

- How can you recognize when you are in a summer season?

- How has one of your difficult seasons shaped your character?

- How has one of your difficult seasons helped you be successful in your summer seasons?

- What perspective on fall and winter has God given you in your summer seasons?

- What kind of attitude have you had toward God during your summer seasons?

Close

Close by praying for each other.

Looking Ahead

Please read Genesis 42:1–24; 50:15–21 for next week.

Journal

Week 5

STORMS~ PRUNING

Breaking UNEXPECTED *unrealistic* expectations *trust* fear *loss of control* danger *character revealing* testing

So now it was not you who sent
me here, but God.

—Genesis 45:8

Introduction to Storms

Storms come upon unexpectedly and suddenly in every season of life. They sweep in to test our character and prune away anything hindering us from the plans God has for us. In the Arizona desert, the worst storms come in July and early August. High winds, heavy rains, lightning strikes, and blinding dust storms are the norm in monsoon season. One summer evening, we watched our neighbors' house burn to the ground after being struck by lightning. Another summer, we had a flash flood with over a foot of rushing water covering our front and back yards.

This July, strong winds broke off tree branches and uprooted trees all across town. For weeks after the storm, we saw cleanup crews removing the damages. The broken tree branches remind me of God's hand. No one likes to clean up debris after a storm, but storms serve a purpose in nature. Our annual monsoon season is by God's design; sometimes we frown at the damage, but we need these storms because they give trees essential pruning.

Our monsoon season is right in the heart of summer—when our trees have grown fast and liberally. New shoots, branches, and leaves expand into the space around them. The hard, wrenching wind bends the branches until they crack and break. Pruning storms test character. The wind breaks off any excess, and the branches that remain are the strong ones. After pruning, the tree is stronger than ever before—and capable of bearing fruit.

God uses storms to break negative traits, habits, thought patterns, and perceptions we develop. He is a careful gardener and shapes us with surgical precision to bear more fruit and come closer to His heart.

Bible Study

- What kind of storm are you most afraid of and why?

- In which seasons do storms occur?

- Name some good things that can come out of a storm?

Review

- What did we learn about summer?

- Where did we leave off in the story of Joseph?

The story of Joseph concludes in his summer season—a season of fruitfulness and success. Eight years into this wonderful season, Joseph encounters a storm (a test.). Storms reveal the depth and strength of the roots. Storms reveal the strength of structures and the quality of their foundations. Storms reveal our character.

In the middle of his summer bliss, Joseph encounters his biggest storm yet. A group of men arrive and betray him. They disown him and send his life on a twenty-year trajectory of slavery and suffering.

Read Genesis 42:1:17.

He puts them in jail for three days.

- What do you think was going through Joseph's heart during those three days?

Read Genesis 42:18–24.

Storms are a cumulative test.

- How is Joseph feeling?

- Who is being tested: Joseph or his brothers?

Read Genesis 43–44.

Joseph's brothers return with Benjamin, and Joseph tests them.

Read Genesis 43:30.

- What does this verse reveal about Joseph's heart toward his brothers?

- Is this a man who is bitter and revengeful?

Read Genesis 44:33.

- Do you see a change in Joseph's brothers?

- Have their hearts changed?

Read Genesis 44:33–34.

Judah begs to be taken as a slave instead of Benjamin.

- What does this reveal about Judah's heart?

Read Genesis 45:1–11.

"So now it was not you who sent me here, but God" (Genesis 45:8).

Joseph was thirty-nine years old, and it was twenty-two years after he first had his dreams.

- What character traits were revealed in Joseph through this storm? Forgiveness, humility, trust, wisdom, discernment, love, a soft heart, a heart free from bitterness, kindness, and hope.

- What attributes impress you most about Joseph in this storm? Why?

- Why was this final storm needed in Joseph's life?

- How would the story have ended differently if Joseph had been bitter or revengeful toward his brothers?

- What things were broken off or pruned in Joseph's life during this storm?

Conclusion

Read Genesis 50:15–21.

- How does verse 20 reveal the kind of man Joseph has become?

Read Genesis 50:26.

Joseph dies at age 110, and he stays faithful to God to the very end of his life.

Storm Response Questions

Discuss in groups of three)

- What stands out to you the most in the story of Joseph?

- Have you had any storms where some of your exposed character traits were not ideal? What were they?

- Share a storm you have gone through and some positive character traits it brought out in you.

- Joseph had to forgive his brothers for causing twenty years of suffering. Is there anyone in your life who you have forgiven or need to forgive for causing great harm or suffering to you?

Close

Close by praying for each other and any storms you are going through.

Looking Ahead

Next week will begin the final three sessions of our study, which include creating a personal timeline. There is no homework for next week.

Journal

Week 6

YOUR SEASONS~ CREATING A TIMELINE

Processing understanding

CHARACTER GROWTH lies exposed

healing *insight* clarity *life lessons*

Introduction to Your Seasons

Psalm 105 recounts the story of the nation of Israel and includes Joseph's story as one small part in God's grand plan. Psalm 105:1–2 says, "Give praise to the Lord, proclaim his name; make known among the nations what he has done. Sing to him, sing praise to him; tell of all his wonderful acts" (NIV). Psalm 105:5 says, "Remember the wonders he has done, his miracles, and the judgments he pronounced" (NIV).

In Psalm 105, King David is telling the story of Joseph and detailing the amazing miracles God did in bringing the Israelites (Joseph's family and descendants) out of Egypt. God also wants us to recall our own stories and share them. God is proud when we share our lives with others and recount the highs and lows of recognizing His faithful and loving hand on our circumstances. When we share our stories, God's goodness shines. We will conclude our *Seasons of a Woman's Soul* study in the next two weeks with recalling, sharing, and reflecting on our personal stories.

Today, we begin to tie the lessons learned in the amazing story of Joseph to our own lives. In the final chapters of Genesis, we saw the remarkable conclusion Joseph came to as he was able to process all his suffering and see God's loving hand bringing good and saving him and his entire family.

In Genesis 50:20, Joseph says to his brothers, "You intended to harm me, but God intended it for good to accomplish what is now being done, the saving of many lives" (NIV). Joseph was able to see that God had a bigger plan than just Joseph's own life and comfort. God wonderfully redeemed all of Joseph's pain and confusion. God brought Joseph to the exalted position where he was able to save his entire family, including all those who had made him suffer.

Our suffering is not always about us. God uses it for a greater good and a higher purpose. Our personal pain will be turned around and used to help save, comfort, and heal others. Today, we begin the process of examining our own lives. We will look at our major life events and pray for the Holy Spirit to show us the story of redemption and beauty God is weaving through our journeys. God doesn't waste our suffering. He is weaving and tying our life experiences together for a positive purpose: for our own benefit and for the benefit of others. Our personal suffering isn't always about us; often, like in Joseph's life, it is about God planning a greater good that will help and benefit many people.

Today, you will create and share your timeline with the other women in your group. Spend about ten minutes creating your timeline. Everyone will have about twenty minutes to share with the group. Half the women will share this week, and half will share next week. You will not have time to detail every major event in your life. Your aim should be to recall and write down only the most life-impacting events.

You will absolutely love hearing the heartbreaking and God-inspiring details of each other's stories. Next week (week 7) our Bible study will continue with sharing the timelines, and the final week concludes with processing and reflecting on those timelines. God will bring you revelations and show you how He has used your suffering for good and how your losses and low points led you toward new and wonderful seasons of your life.

Ask the Holy Spirit to help you remember the significant events in your life and for God to open your eyes to see the redemptive good He is working in and through your story.

Creating Your Timeline

- You have about ten minutes to create your timeline. This exercise is not intended to record all the significant events in your life. It will focus on a handful of events you will examine more thoroughly.
- Create a timeline beginning at zero up to your current age. As you fill out events from your life, put all positive events above your timeline. Record the events vertically based on the size of the impact they had on your life. The most significant events should be recorded up high on your paper, and the events with smaller impacts will be near the center horizontal line. Record negative events below your line. Just like the positive events, delineate the level of impact each event had on your life by drawing line shorter or longer lines. Please answer the questions and record the following events on your timeline:

- (Summer) Joseph's first positive impact was receiving his coat of many colors from his father and having God-given dreams of greatness. To begin your timeline, write down any childhood dreams or ambitions.
- (Fall) Joseph experiences tragedy as his brothers sell him into slavery. Record any tragedy or loss you have experienced.
- (Storm) Joseph is falsely accused by Potiphar's wife and is thrown into prison. Have you experienced any injustice?
- (Winter) Joseph may have wrestled with intense emotions after being thrown into prison unjustly. Record any seasons of bitterness, anger, or confusion.
- (Spring) Record the times you were abandoned, overlooked, or forgotten?
- (Summer) Joseph was released from prison and promoted to second-in-command over all of Egypt. Write down any awards, promotions, or recognition you have received.
- (Summer) Joseph ruled with God's wisdom and excellence—storing grain away during the seven years of plenty. Record any seasons where things were going well for you and you felt like you were hitting your stride or in your element.

- (Storms) In the middle of ruling the land of Egypt and wisely distributing grain, Joseph encounters an unexpected test when his brothers arrive. Write down any storms you have been through (financial, health, relational, crisis of faith, etc.).

Timeline

Timeline

Close

Close by getting in groups of three people and praying for each other.

Looking Ahead

You will have a chance to finish hearing the timelines next week and begin digging deeper into your main life events. There is no homework for next week.

Journal

Week 7

YOUR SEASONS~ PROCESSING

Revelation HEALING clarity
understanding insight **peace**

The path of the righteous is like the morning sun, shining ever brighter till the full light of day.

—Proverbs 4:18

Introduction

Begin this session by finishing up the timeline sharing. Every woman should have fifteen or twenty minutes to share their timeline. When the last person has finished sharing, take ten minutes to read and write down the answers to the questions below. After everyone has completed the questions, you will share and discuss your answers. This is your second-to-last week. If you don't finish processing your timeline, you can carry some questions over to the final week.

Today is a special time. The Holy Spirit is going to bring you a brand-new perspective on your past and bring healing to your hearts. Your heavenly Father wants to reveal His love to you in greater ways as you reflect, share, and process.

Life is so busy, and we have very little time for reflection. Today you have time to seek God's perspective on your past. Don't rush this process—enjoy it! Pray for revelation and for the Holy Spirit to open your eyes. God has been at work in your life. You have a beautiful story to tell. Your story brings glory to God and shines his goodness to all who hear it. As you share your story with others, you will begin to understand more of it yourself.

Proverbs 4:18 says, "The path of the righteous is like the morning sun, shining ever brighter till the full light of day." It's like looking out your window just before sunrise and watching the shadowy outlines of trees and bushes slowly coming into focus as the sun rises. We will experience this clarity as we invite God into our time of processing and reflecting. Help others see God in their stories, and they will help you see God's goodness in your life as well.

Processing Your Timeline

- Use colored pens to mark your different seasons—
  or you can draw different shapes around them.
  Look back over your timeline:

  o Put a red circle around any fall seasons. Fall is
    a season of transition or loss.
  o Put a blue box around any winter seasons you
    find. Winter is a time of rest or unseen growth.
  o Put a pink heart around your spring seasons.
    Spring is a season of hope and investing.
  o Put a green star by your summer seasons.
    Summer is a season of fruitfulness—when you
    are living your dream.
  o Put a black zigzag by your storms. Storms are
    the season of pruning and testing.

Here is an example of what Joseph's timeline could
look like:

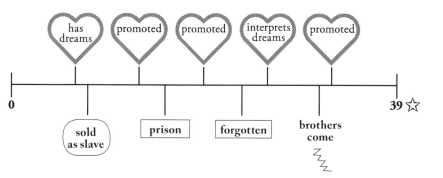

- Look at your fall and winter seasons:

  o What healthy character traits were being formed in you through these experiences?

  o What negative traits were exposed in you?

  o What misconceptions about who God is did you let go of?

  o What truths replaced them?

- Look at your spring and summer seasons:

  o What beliefs about yourself were being formed during these times?

  o Were any negative traits exposed in you through your success?

- o How did your spring and summer seasons shape your concept of who God is?

- Share a storm you experienced and how your trust in God helped you through it.

Close

Get in groups of three people and pray for each other for continued revelation from the Holy Spirit on our timelines this week.

Looking Ahead

Next week concludes our *Seasons of a Woman's Soul* study. There is no homework.

Journal

Week 8

YOUR SEASONS~ REFLECTION AND CELEBRATION

Thankfulness *praise* **celebration**

sharing GOD'S GOODNESS God's

faithfulness joy *the big picture*

life story *testimony*

Sing to him, sing praise to him; tell
of all his wonderful acts. Glory in
his holy name; let the hearts of
those who seek the Lord rejoice.
—Psalm 105:2–3 NIV

Give thanks to Him and praise
His name! For the Lord is good
and His love is eternal, and
His faithfulness endures to all
generations.
—Psalm 100:5 NIV

Introduction

Understanding and telling our stories is one of the most
powerful ways we can communicate God's goodness to
others. We bring Him great pleasure as we shine who He
is to the world around us. Before we can share our stories,
we need to understand them ourselves and see God's hand
of faithfulness through them all.

Through our times of processing and reflecting, God
brings healing and greater clarity to our past. We see,
often for the first time, how God was there through all
our ups and downs and how He was shaping our character
and developing our concept of who He really is. Above
all, we see God's goodness, faithfulness, and incredible

plan unfold. We get to share our amazing stories of God's goodness with the world around us.

Today, you will share your final insights from your life story and have the opportunity to celebrate the incredible goodness of God in all our lives!

Review

- Who can summarize the five seasons of the soul we covered in this study?

Final Reflection Questions

- What season of growth do you think you are in now? Why?

- How does knowing that God has a purpose for each season help us?

- How has God used your fall transition seasons to shape your location or vocation?

- Joseph came to realize much of his suffering was needed to position him for a bigger purpose. His slavery and imprisonment were necessary to save an entire nation from famine and preserve the lineage of Christ! Can you think of something you have been through that God used for good in other's lives?

- How can you summarize your life story in three or four sentences to communicate God's faithfulness to others?

- Joseph finishes his life with a heart of forgiveness, kindness, love, and a deep trust in God's purposes. What kind of person will you be at ninety years old?

- What things need to happen in order for you to stay on this trajectory and finish life well?

Close

Close by having everyone pray out prayers of praise and thankfulness for God's goodness.

Secrets for Creating an Amazing Small Group

Real Answers

I simply asked the ladies who just finished going through our *Seasons of a Woman's Soul* study what they really liked about our group. Here are their answers with a few added comments from me.

On and Off Ramps

My small group has met weekly for ten years. The group has a handful of original members, and many ladies have joined us in more recent years, including just a few months ago. I allow the group to ebb and flow. That is how life is. I don't think anyone would have signed up for the first group if I had announced it was a ten-year commitment! Too much commitment scares people away. I like to ask for shorter commitments and a set amount of time.

Each study has an ending point. It is like driving on the interstate—we all need places to easily exit if needed. I allow ladies to come and go with grace and love. Everyone attending my group has had a season of attending the study and a season when they needed to step back and do other things.

Once or twice a year, I begin a new study and invite everyone to join. I offer a continual highway of studies for those who want to continue meeting. Be a road map by letting the ladies know what is up next. I ask for suggestions for the next study topic, and we decide together what we will study next.

This morning, we finished our last session of the *Seasons of a Woman's Soul* study. Next week, we will gather again for a Christmas brunch and a gift exchange. We won't meet again until January. I don't know who will be joining the study in January—and many of the ladies may not know either—but at least they know the study will continue. The friendships they invested in for eight weeks don't have to end, and they can continue to build on them and enjoy them.

Summary

Set a designated time for your study (such as eight weeks). At the end of the study, offer an exit for those who want to stop and an opportunity to continue to the next study. We always decide what our next study will be before the last day of the original study.

What Makes Our Group So Special?

Have a family meeting up front where you establish ground rules and expectations for the group. Practicing

transparency with each other will create trust and build lifelong relationships.
—Emily S.

I always begin our first meeting with a whiteboard or a large poster board for creating and writing our group core values. I ask the women what they want our group to look like and how we should treat each other. I have someone (with better handwriting than me) write the words on the board, and everyone contributes.

Draw a circle and write the group's core values inside the circle. Also, take a couple minutes to state what we are not—and write those words on the outside of the circle. Here is what our core value board looked like this year:

gossipy

guarded

fun

negative

courageous

loving   encourage

safe   pace   prayer

warrior   transparent

authentic   good listeners

aware   truthful   friends

compassionate

inconsistent   empathetic

disrespecful

fearful

rude   jealous

Have good attendance. Learn through discussion. Grow with others through prayer and encouragement. Create a safe place to share.
—Jenn C.

Aim for weekly attendance—and then live in grace. Life is busy, and people are often overwhelmed. Situations that are beyond our control seem to pop up and prevent attendance. The best thing you can do is do your best to attend every week. Don't schedule a hair appointment or doctor appointment for the same time as group. If you have family visiting, consider bringing them to your group that week. If you can only come for half of group, come late or leave early. Being present for a short time is better than no time at all.

We learn more through discussion than through teaching. Learn from each other. Open your hearts to what other women are saying and learn from their wisdom and the perspectives God has given them. Participate in the discussions. The more you share, the more you will enjoy the study—and the more you will grow.

Pray for each other's needs.
—Linda S.

Be quick to pray for people. Sometimes we need to stop the study in the middle and pray for someone. Be sensitive to people who have heavy hearts and put prayer and encouragement first. Love first, study second. Always close the study time with prayer—but always be ready to pause the study for a time of hugging and prayers if someone's heart is heavy.

Pray for each other outside of group as well. Have each other's contact information and text urgent prayer requests to each other. It's an honor to be asked to pray for each other, and it connects the group to God and one another in deeper ways.

Prayer is like pouring on liquid love. When people open their hearts during group, respond with love, encouragement, and prayer.

Accept people where they are and whatever season they are in.
—Dana B.

You will have diversity in your group. It is wonderful! Celebrate and appreciate the stage where everyone is. Some women have been raised in Christian homes, and some are just learning about who Jesus is and are reading the Bible for the first time. This is exciting! Everyone is welcomed, encouraged, and accepted. Recognize that we are all in different places on the journey to know God.

Sharing the timeline was a wonderful way to practice vulnerability and build and deepen friendships. Having a running text thread is nice for day-to-day communications. An outing like a birthday celebration outside of group is great too!
—Nika D.

Make your group about friendships and not just about the Bible study. Communicate throughout the week. Let other know about prayer requests or if you can't make the group one week. Use a group text thread to communicate warmth, prayer, and appreciation for others. If a text comes to the group that someone is sick and can't attend the study that week, it is wonderful if several people reply that they are praying for a quick return to health and letting them know they will be missed.

Having a running text thread also gives the group ownership and permission to reach out and connect with other women. When the members of the group take on a joint relational responsibility, it takes the relational burden off the group facilitator.

We also like to go out for lunch or dinner once a month to celebrate the birthdays from that month. It is one more way to connect and nurture our friendships.

About the Photographer

Diane Egge is not only my amazing mom—she is a talented photographer. Diane has spent a lifetime capturing nature's majestic elements through her lens. Her many extraordinary photographs of nature were perfect to include in *Seasons of a Woman's Soul*. Each photograph was carefully selected to depict God's beautiful intent for each season in nature and to parallel that beauty in our own lives.

To learn more about Diane Egge and view more of her spectacular photography, visit her at dianeegge.com or on Instagram.

Printed in the United States
By Bookmasters